CREATING A PROFIT SNOWBALL FOR YOUR BUSINESS

How I Find $50K in 50 Minutes in any Business

David Braun

© 2021 ALL RIGHTS RESERVED.

No part of this book may be reproduced or transmitted in any form whatsoever, electronic, or mechanical, including photocopying, recording, or by any informational storage or retrieval system without the expressed written, dated and signed permission from the author.

LIMITS OF LIABILITY / DISCLAIMER OF WARRANTY:

The author and publisher of this book have used their best efforts in preparing this material. While every attempt has been made to verify information provided in this book, neither the author nor the publisher assumes any responsibility for any errors, omissions or inaccuracies.

The author and publisher make no representation or warranties with respect to the accuracy, applicability, fitness, or completeness of the contents of this program. They disclaim any warranties (expressed or implied), merchantability, or fitness for any purpose. The author and publisher shall in no event be held liable for any loss or other damages, including but not limited to special, incidental, consequential, or other damages. As always, the advice of a competent legal, tax, accounting or other professional should be sought.

To Svea, my beautiful wife & partner in life... and to all my life mentors for the invaluable wisdom shared with me.

Table of Contents

Introduction

   How I Find $50K in 50 Minutes
   For Small Business Owners 1

Chapter 1

   Understanding the Snowball Effect 5

Chapter 2

   Creating Your Market Dominating Position 7

Chapter 3

   Creating a Powerful Offer 15

Chapter 4

   Marketing and Advertising 25

Chapter 5

   Joint Ventures................................... 41

Chapter 6

   Downselling...................................... 47

Chapter 7

    Drip Campaigns 51

Chapter 8

    Upsell / Cross-sell 63

Chapter 9

    Expand Products or Service Offerings.............. 73

Chapter 10

    Bundling.. 77

Chapter 11

    Increase Pricing 83

Chapter 12

    What the 1% Know................................. 87

INTRODUCTION

How I Find $50K in 50 Minutes For Small Business Owners

The purpose of this book is to walk you through a process I've created where I find any business a minimum of $50,000 in just 50 minutes.

I'll go through several simple strategies which are proven revenue-generators for any small business. Most business owners know nothing about these strategies, and therefore, are failing to capitalize on their revenue-generating power.

For the purposes of this book, I'll cover each of these strategies in individual chapters for one main reason. I want you to be able to review these strategies and minimize the amount of time it will take you to implement them in their entirety.

But consider this, most business owners today are in the fight of their lives. Most of them have no additional revenue sources they can tap into for financial support during lean times – and their marketing and advertising aren't working as well as they used to. In fact, for many small business owners, marketing isn't producing any results for them at all, and their financial situation is growing more desperate by the day.

As a business owner or entrepreneur, if you're struggling right now to generate more leads and clients for your business, and you need to find immediate ways to dramatically increase your business' bottom-line revenue, then spend the next few minutes reading this and I'll show you how we can help you make all of these problems disappear forever.

Small business owners are desperate for proven and tested ways to generate more leads, attract more clients, and make more money. So, what if I told you that I can show you how to generate all the leads business owners need in order to completely dominate their market? What if I could prove to you right now we can find ANY small business owner more than $50,000 in additional revenue, and do it in just 50 minutes?

Over the next few chapters, I'm going to give you back door access to a series of powerful business growth strategies that are some of the most powerful revenue-generating strategies ever created. But first, I need to explain the amazing results of what happens when these strategies combine using the snowball effect. Are you ready? Let's get reading.

CHAPTER 1

Understanding the Snowball Effect

I remember as a child being inspired the first time, I watched a cartoon showing the snowball effect. The snowball effect describes the process of a small ball of snow rolling down a snow-covered hill, increasing in size and speed by attracting the snow it rolls over. Recognized in a variety of fields (i.e. computer sciences, leadership studies, etc.), visualized in entertainment and referred to in business, this snowball effect leads to powerful outcomes.

To successfully execute the strategies presented in this book, it's helpful for you to understand the potential the snowball effect has on your bottom line. When you combine more than one of the fundamental strategies listed in this book, you will unlock your businesses exponential profit and impact potential.

To highlight the snowball effect, let's look at the 1 penny riddle. If you doubled 1 penny every day for a month, how much money would you have after thirty days? Well, after 4 days you might have 8 cents and after 2 weeks, the total would be $81.92. Not very impressive... right? Well, by the 18th day, your penny would be at $1 301.72. On the 24th day your penny would have grown to $83 866.08. By the 30th day your final total would amount to $5 368 709.12.

The dramatic daily accelerated growth of your penny is based on the increase of each new day's larger sum, not on your original penny. This example highlights the power of compounding impacts... the results are not about adding up different impacts but rather about multiplying the impacts with each other. The results are really quite exciting and often surprise my clients.

Applying the strategies in this book to your business will multiply your profitability. As you add each new strategy, the combined impact snowballs because each new strategy is magnified by the impact of other strategies you have already implemented. The result is a snowball effect. The surprising thing is rarely if ever, have I found a small business which has implemented these fundamental strategies in effective ways. So let's check out these strategies and see how you can create your own profit snowball.

CHAPTER 2

Creating Your Market Dominating Position

To successfully execute the strategies presented in this book, it's imperative you have certain fundamentals in place. These are fundamentals will separate your business from your competition and give you a competitive edge.

So, let's start by helping you establish a market dominating position for your business. The majority of businesses are established in response to market demand for a product or service. Many build their businesses by serving that demand and enjoy growing profits without putting much effort into long-term planning or marketing.

However, what happens when demand slows or stops? What happens when the competition sets up shop with a "new and improved" version of your product down the road? How do you keep your offering fresh while growing and maintaining your client base? The answer - innovate your business and offer extraordinary value by creating a "market dominating position."

Consider this. Every choice you make when buying a product or a service represents a point of differentiation between one company and their competitors. These differences, whether subtle or distinct, determine which customers will buy what they sell.

Take the well-documented case of Domino's Pizza as an example. Why did Dominos become a billion-dollar behemoth in an overcrowded market in just a few years? Did Dominos make the best pizza? No. Did they offer comfortable in-house dining? No. Did they offer the largest selection on their menu? No. They pretty much offered the SAME PIZZA as all of their competitors!

They dominated by adopting and implementing one major strategy. They created a market dominating position in an area with lots of colleges, which was fast, hot pizza targeted specifically to hungry college kids.

Ask yourself what, if anything, makes your business different from your competitors as perceived by your targeted

CHAPTER 2: CREATING YOUR MARKET DOMINATING POSITION

prospects and customers? For the vast majority of businesses the answer is price.

Many years ago, Nike offered the top-selling Air Jordan 3 for $150. At the exact same time, Target sold an excellent imitation of the Air Jordan for around $40, but Nike outsold them, ten to one.

Starbucks is a popular place to buy coffee in many parts of the world. According to the latest data, their typical customer spends four times more than they would at their competitors.

Obviously, low price isn't the driving force here. So, what is? The answer - these companies staked out a specific and targeted market dominating position. Nike focused their position around being the best athlete, being hip and in style, along with the perception of quality. Starbucks focused on delicious hand-crafted beverages which they claimed is the secret to making life better. Avis is number 2 so they try harder. FedEx is for people who absolutely, positively have to have it there overnight. And the list goes on.

When you create your own market dominating position, you will consistently get businesses and individuals to choose your business over your competitors.

But what exactly is a "market dominating position"? It's simply any value-added customer perceived benefit, or a combination of benefits, which differentiates you from your competitors, and does so in a strong enough manner it makes your business the logical choice in the minds of your prospects and customers.

As an example, a dry cleaner who offers pick-up and delivery would be the only logical choice for any prospect or customer who values convenience. This simple distinction represents a market dominating position.

The key is to create added value in everything you do. Prospects and customers DON'T buy based on price; they buy based on the value they receive for the price they pay. Creating added value is a marketing or customer relations strategy that can take the form of a product or service that's added to your original offering for free or as part of a discounted package.

Like all other elements in your marketing toolkit, it's designed to attract new customers and retain existing ones. Another simple example of added value is a gift shop owner offering complimentary gift wrapping with every purchase.

If you don't revisit the value you offer, then over time your customers will be drawn to a competitor who consistently innovates their business, so they offer exceptional value you don't. Ultimately your customers will demand

CHAPTER 2: CREATING YOUR MARKET DOMINATING POSITION

additional value for them to remain loyal – and they're the keystones for your business growth.

Everyone can add value to their business. And adding value doesn't have to blow your marketing budget or take up hours of your time. There are many ways to enhance your business.

The key to adding value is determining what your customers and target market perceive as valuable. You must understand their needs, wants, troubles, and inconveniences in order to entice them with solutions through added value products or services.

Adding value will also add to your profits. However, if you don't focus on genuinely helping your clients, you'll have a difficult time attracting them.

Added value works for both product and service-based businesses. If you offer a service like hairstyling, try treating your customers by offering them a latte while they wait, or complimentary shampoo samples, or a free conditioning treatment with every sixth visit.

If you sell a product, consider offering convenience services like free shipping or delivery to make the customer's experience a seamless one.

The customer will feel appreciated, and their needs will have been taken care of. The online retailer Zappos.com built a billion-dollar behemoth with this strategy.

DIFFERENTIATING YOUR BUSINESS FROM COMPETITORS

Differentiating your business from your competitors by creating a market dominating position (MDP) involves a five-step process.

Step 1: Determine your strategic position in the market.

What specific niche market or segment of the marketplace should your business focus on? Determining this involves combining the skills your business has with the unmet needs of your targeted prospects, and then designing your product or service to fulfill those needs.

Domino's strategic position was "fast, hot pizza for hungry college kids." For Starbucks, "delicious hand-crafted beverages that makes life better."

Step 2: Determine your primary MDP.

This is the most dominating advantage that separates you from your competitors. Domino's Pizza claimed it could deliver its pizza in 30 minutes or less, or they would give it to you for FREE! This was the primary advantage that met the needs of their newly defined market position - hungry college kids who wanted food fast.

Step 3: Determine your supporting business model.

How will you specifically deliver what your strategic position and primary market dominating position promises? What changes, if any, do you need to consider making to your business to ensure you deliver consistently on your position and your promise?

Domino's Pizza built a supporting business model enabling them to consistently provide their promised primary advantage – fresh, hot pizza delivered within 30 minutes.

To make good on this promise every time, they were forced to create a supporting business model where they built low-cost, plain-vanilla stores strategically located near college campuses.

And since college kids aren't the most reliable workers on the planet, they were forced to hire additional delivery staff and have additional drivers on a stand-by basis. Together, these innovations allowed them to consistently meet and often exceed their primary market dominating position.

Step 4: Determine a secondary MDP.

What additional competitive advantages does your business offer that your customers will perceive as being different from your competition? Domino's secondary benefits might include special pricing, assorted sizes, a much broader selection of toppings, or additional menu items.

Step 5: Create your MDP statement or elevator pitch.

This is a simple statement you can create by combining steps one through four. This helps you to state unequivocally what differentiates you from your competitors to your targeted prospects and customers.

Domino's market dominating position is neatly summed up in its slogan, "fresh, hot pizza delivered in 30 minutes or less or it's free."

Now we need to define your market dominating position, and then we can help create a powerful and compelling elevator pitch that will effectively communicate your value to your marketplace.

CHAPTER 3

Creating a Powerful Offer

I'm not going to beat around the bush on this one:

Your offer is the granite foundation of your marketing campaign.

Get it right, and everything else will fall into place. Your headline will grab readers, your copy will sing, your ad layout will hardly matter, and you will have customers running to your door or website.

Get it wrong, and even the best looking, best written campaign will sink like the Titanic.

A powerful offer is an irresistible offer. It's an offer that gets your audience frothing at the mouth and clamoring over each other all the way to your door. An offer that makes your readers pick up the phone and open their wallets.

Irresistible offers make your potential customers think, "I'd be crazy not to take him up on that", or "An offer like this doesn't come around very often." They instill a sense of emotion, of desire, and ultimately, urgency.

Make it easy for customers to purchase from you the first time, and spend your time keeping them coming back.

I'll say it again: **get it right, and everything else will fall into place.**

The Crux of Your Marketing Campaign

As you work your way through this program, you will find virtually every chapter discusses the importance of a powerful offer as related to your marketing strategy or promotional campaign.

There's a reason for this. The powerful offer is more often than not the reason a customer will open their wallets. It is how you generate leads, and then convert them into loyal customers. The more dramatic, unbelievable, and valuable the offer is the more dramatic and unbelievable the response will be.

Many companies spend thousands of dollars on impressive marketing campaigns on television and in social media ads. They send massive direct mail campaigns on a regular basis; yet don't receive an impressive or massive response rate.

These companies do not yet understand, simply providing information on their company and the benefit of their product is not enough to get prospects to act. There is no reason to visit the store or website *right now*.

Your powerful, irresistible offer can:

- Increase leads
- Drive traffic to your website or business
- Move old product
- Convert leads into customers
- Build your customer database

What Makes a Powerful Offer?

A powerful offer is one that makes the most people respond and take action. It gets people running to spend money on your product or service.

Powerful offers nearly always have an element of *urgency* and of *scarcity*. They give your audience a reason to act immediately, instead of putting it off until a later date.

Urgency relates to time. The offer is only available until a certain date, during a certain period of the day, or if you act within a few hours of seeing the ad. The customer needs to act now to take advantage of the offer. Think Amazon Prime Days as an example.

Scarcity related to quantity. There are only a certain number of customers who will be able to take advantage of the offer. There may be a limited number of spaces, a limited number of products, or simply a limited number of people the business will provide the offer to. Again, this requires customer to act immediately to reap the high value for low cost.

Powerful offers also:

Offer great value.

Customers perceive the offer as having great value – more than a single product on its own, or the product at its regular price. It is clear the offer takes the reader's needs and wants into consideration.

Make sense to the reader.

They are simple and easy to understand if read quickly. Avoid percentages – use half-off or 2-for-1 instead of 50% off. There are no "catches" or requirements, no fine print.

Seem logical.

The offer doesn't come out of thin air. There is a logical reason behind it – a holiday, end of season, anniversary celebration, or new product. People can get suspicious of offers that seem "too good to be true" and have no apparent purpose.

Provide a premium.

The offer provides something extra to the customer, like a free gift, or free product or service. They feel they are getting something extra for no extra cost. Premiums are perceived to have more value than discounts.

Remember when your target market reads your offer, they will be asking the following questions:

1. What are you offering me?

2. What's in it for me?

3. What makes me sure I can believe you?

4. How much do I have to pay for it?

The Most Powerful Types of Offers

Decide what kind of offer will most effectively achieve your objectives. Are you trying to generate leads, convert customers, build a database, move old product off the shelves, or increase sales?

Consider what type of offer will be of most value to your ideal customers – what offer will make them act quickly.

Free Offer

This type of offer asks customers to act immediately in exchange for something free. This is a good strategy to use to build a customer database or mailing list. Offer a free consultation, free consumer report, or other item of low cost to you but of high perceived value.

You can also advertise the value of the item you are offering for free. For example, act now and you'll receive a free consultation worth $75. This will dramatically increase your lead generation, and allow you to focus on conversion when the customer comes through the door or visits your website.

The Value Added Offer

Add additional services or products that cost you very little, and combine them with other items to increase their attractiveness. This increases the perception of value in the prospect's mind, which will justify increasing the price of a product or service without incurring extra hard costs to your business.

Package Offer

Package your products or services together in a logical way to increase the perceived value as a whole. Discount the value of the package by a small margin, and position it as a "start-up kit" or "special package." By packaging goods of mixed values, you will be able to close more high-value sales. For example: including a free desk-jet printer with every computer purchase.

Premium Offer

Offer a bonus product or service with the purchase of another. This strategy will serve your bottom line much better than discounting. This includes 2-for-1 offers, offers including free gifts, and in-store credit with purchases over a specific dollar amount.

Urgency Offer

As I mentioned above, offers including an element of urgency enjoy a better response rate, as there is a reason for your customers to act immediately. Give the offer a deadline or limit the number of spots available.

Guarantee Offer

Offer to take away the risk of making a purchase from your customers. Guarantee the performance or results of your product or service, and offer to compensate the customer with their money back if they are not satisfied. This will help overcome any fear or reservations about your product, and make it more likely for your leads to become customers.

Create Your Powerful Offer

Pick a single product or service.

Focus on only one product or service – or one product or service *type* – at a time. This will keep your offer clear, simple, and easy to understand. This can be an area of your business you wish to grow, or old product that you need to move off the shelves.

Decide what you want your customers to do.

What are you looking to achieve from your offer? If it is to generate more leads, then you'll need your customer to contact you. If it is to quickly sell old product, you'll need your customer to come into the store and buy it. Do you want them to visit your website? Sign up for your newsletter? How long do they have to act? Be clear about your call to action, and state it clearly in your offer.

Dream up the biggest, best offer.

First, think of the biggest, best things you could offer your customers – regardless of cost and ability. Don't limit yourself to a single type of offer, combine several types of offers to increase value. Offer a premium, plus a guarantee, with a package offer. Then take a look at what you've created, and make the necessary changes so it is realistic.

Run the numbers.

Finally, make sure the offer will leave you with some profit – or at least allow you to break even. You don't want to publish an outrageous offer that will generate a tremendous number of leads, but leave you broke. Remember that each customer has an acquisition cost, as well as a lifetime value. The amount of their first purchase may allow you to break even, but the amount of their subsequent purchases may make you a lovely profit.

CHAPTER 4

Marketing and Advertising

Let's face it. The major hot button for most small businesses these days is the ability to generate leads. All small businesses want more leads, but few of them know how to successfully attract customers to their business.

As a coach, I have in-depth knowledge and skill when it comes to generating leads. So, here's the process I use to do this.

If you're like 99% of the business owners I speak with, you may often feel lost or overwhelmed as you try to navigate through all the various options available these days. Websites, social media, SEO, email marketing, Facebook, pay-per-click, and so on.

Let me do you a favor right now and completely remove that overwhelm from your life forever. Are you familiar with the 80/20 rule?

For business owners, it means 20% of what you do every day is generating 80% of your total annual revenue.

In other words, you're only doing a few things daily to make most of your money. I can tell you specifically what makes up that 20%, and it's all you really need to focus on after today.

Remember I told you I'm going to find you more than $100,000 in less than 45 minutes by reading this book?

I'm going to do that by focusing on just 2 or 3 areas, so you can imagine what you could actually generate revenue-wise if you implemented all the areas of your business.

Most business owners would KILL to almost double their revenue, wouldn't you agree?

Your business could skyrocket from $62,500 to almost half a million dollars annually with small subtle changes in a small number of areas in your business.

When asked, most business owners tell me "word of mouth", or more often than not "referrals", are how they generate leads. Referrals are obviously an excellent lead source. In fact, it may be the best one by far, but the problem is you never know when you will get them. They're not reliable and you certainly can't generate them whenever you want.

99% of businesses today do have a website. Do you know for sure how many leads your website generates every month? Do you know for sure how many sales your website produces every month?

Can I show you why your website isn't generating leads or closing sales for you? In fact, would you like for me to give you the deeply hidden secrets that the marketing gurus DON'T want you to know?

Here's the key to successful marketing. You MUST be able to enter the conversation taking place in the head of your prospects. Or another way to look at it is to be able to address the number one question on your prospect's mind at just the right time. So how do you do this? It's actually quite simple when you know and understand the fundamentals of marketing.

The conversation that's taking place in EVERY prospect's mind revolves around two major points. There's a problem they have and don't want, and there's a result they want but don't have.

Now, believe it or not, there is actually a marketing formula we follow that takes these two points into account and spits out a message so compelling it practically forces your prospects to buy what you sell.

It's called the Conversion Equation, and it looks like this – Interrupt, Engage, Educate and Offer. The Interrupt is your headline – which means it's the first thing someone sees when they visit your website, read any of your marketing collateral, or hear you speak. When someone asks you what you do, it's the first words out of your mouth. That's your headline and it MUST address the problem your prospects have and don't want.

The Engage is your sub-headline – which is the second thing your prospects see or hear. It MUST address the result your prospect wants but doesn't have. The Educate is the information you provide - either verbally or in writing - that presents evidence to your prospects you and your product or service are superior in every way to your competition.

Unfortunately, MOST businesses aren't different from their competitors, and that's why you MUST innovate your business to create what we refer to as a market dominating position.

You MUST make your business unique. It MUST stand out from the crowd. It MUST make your prospects say to themselves they would be absolute idiots to buy from anyone else but you – regardless of price. And finally, the

Offer. You MUST create a compelling offer that makes it so irresistible your prospects can't turn it down.

But here's another critical fundamental of marketing. Because of the saturation of marketing messages these days, most prospects have become numb to most marketing.

Following our Conversion Equation can dramatically overcome this, but even with this powerful tool in play, it will still take multiple "touch" points before your prospects will buy what you sell.

For most businesses today, it takes anywhere from 20 to more than 100 touch points before a prospect makes their buying decision. Following the Conversion Equation reduces the touch points to somewhere between 5 to 12 points of contact.

But here's the key, most businesses don't follow up with their prospects at all, and this provides a HUGE window of opportunity for ANY business that does follow up - to position themselves as the dominant force in their industry.

But, in order to have the opportunity to get your message in front of your prospects 5 to 12 times, you MUST find a way to collect their contact information, and that's the purpose of your Offer.

Most businesses offer something that only appeals to prospects we call NOW buyers – prospects ready to make an immediate purchase. Unfortunately, NOW buyers make up less than 1% of the total number of prospects who are in the market to buy what you sell.

These businesses typically offer prospects a free consultation, a discount, a coupon, a free assessment, a complimentary quote, or the biggest mistake of all... CALL US!

For most businesses, all of their marketing material – website, digital ads, business card, etc. - all list their phone number as their sole offer which ONLY appeals to that 1% of NOW buyers. The remaining 99% of viable prospects are "investigating" and gathering information about what you sell.

They're searching for information because they want to determine who is offering the best value. You see, prospects DON'T shop price – they shop VALUE!

The only reason prospects consider price is most businesses don't give them any other value proposition to consider except price.

Remember what I said a moment ago about making your business unique – creating a market-dominating position?

Most businesses don't do that, and since they and all of their competitors look exactly the same, prospects are FORCED to shop price. So, with these fundamentals in mind, let's see how your website stacks up to them.

Let me show you a website we just revised for a child psychologist so you can see what I mean, and then let's take a look at your website as a comparison. Here is a child psychologist's original website.

This is typical for this industry, and 99% of his colleagues' websites look EXACTLY like this. Notice the generic headline – Parenting Advice and Resources from Dr. John Smith.

He has to have a headline like that because he's attempting to be all things to all prospects. Basically, this doctor helps parents deal with adolescent problems. Look at the 9 areas he services – emotionally disturbed kids, behavioral problems, teen pregnancy, peer pressure and so on.

So, let's compare this site with the fundamentals we just discussed. First, you MUST create a market-dominating position. This doctor could actually create 9 of them by simply positioning his specialty in each of his 9 individual areas of treatment.

For example, let's say he decides to start with the top condition on his list... emotionally disturbed kids. These are kids that yell, scream and constantly have a highly belligerent attitude toward their parents. They scream at them and are known in some cases to threaten the parents. These kids can't be reasoned with and these poor parents have NO clue how to deal with this situation.

So, here's what this doctor needs to do. Forget the website completely – this doctor needs what is known as a squeeze page. This is a single page online specifically addressing ONLY this one condition. So, what should this page look like and what should it say?

Remember the second fundamental – you MUST enter the conversation taking place in the head of your prospect. There's a problem they have and don't want and there's a result they want but don't have. This is where we implement the first two components of the Conversion Equation – Interrupt and Engage. The headline is the Interrupt, and it must address the problem they have and don't want.

Here's the squeeze page we created for this doctor that did that.

Notice the headline – "Are You Sick and Tired of The Yelling, Screaming and Belligerent Attitude of Your Child?" Does that address the problem these parents have and don't want? Would you say that's a 100% bullseye?

Now, for the Engage which is the sub-headline. It MUST address the result they want but don't have. Notice it says – "Now You Can Discover the Secrets to Controlling Your Child and Instantly Restore Peace and Quiet in Your Home." Would you say that's bullseye number two?

Now, let's look at the third Conversion Equation component Educate. In the doctor's original website, because he's trying to appeal to all prospects, his video said this – "Greeting parents. I want to welcome you to remarkable parenting. You will find tons of great information here with hundreds of pages of articles."

Think how ridiculous this sounds if I'm one of these parents with a kid who has a belligerent attitude. Do I want to read hundreds of pages of articles? Or am I searching for a specific solution to a specific problem? Do you see why most websites these days are basically a total and complete waste of money? They don't address the things your prospects are truly looking for. Here's the new script we created for this doctor.

"As a parent, are you struggling to gain control of your child's attitude and emotions? Is your child yelling and screaming at you, while often displaying a belligerent and sometimes threatening tone that no matter what you do or try you just can't seem to get under control?

"My name is Dr. John Smith, and I help parents like you every day learn the techniques that will solve these frustrating and destructive behavioral patterns once and for all. In fact, let me prove it to you. Enter your first name and email in the box to the right, and I'll send you a series of 60-second techniques that will immediately restore peace and quiet in your home."

Think that just might get more prospects to respond to this message? And that brings us to the final component of the Conversion Equation... the Offer. Look at the doctor's original offer. It was for a free consultation. The only prospects that will accept that type of offer are those NOW buyers. Remember, they make up less than 1% of the total number of prospects looking for this type of help.

When your offer is to "call me," that basically says "let me sell you" to your prospects. We are so used to getting non-stop sales pitches these days we resist calling anyone with every fiber of our being. Most people won't answer their phone unless they recognize the caller ID. This type of offer is called an incentive offer, and incentive offers only work for common purchases, emergency situations, and impulse purchases.

And remember, most prospects don't buy until they have been exposed to your messaging somewhere between 5 to 12 times. If you tell prospects to "call you", and most won't, how do you keep marketing to them? Obviously, you can't. The secret to effective marketing is to offer what most prospects truly want... INFORMATION!

Look at the last sentence in the child psychologist's video script - "enter your first name and email in the box to the right, and I'll send you a series of 60 second techniques that will immediately restore peace and quiet in your home." That offer is ZERO risk to a prospect, and it offers them something they truly want... a <u>solution</u> to their problem.

They can receive it by simply providing their name and email address WITHOUT having to speak to anyone or be subjected to any type of sales pitch. That's why the offer on this doctor's squeeze page says, "Learn the Secrets to Gaining and Maintaining Complete Control of Your Child in Less than 60 Seconds." Is that a highly compelling offer that would appeal to a majority of the prospects directed to this page?

And do you now see why we call this a squeeze page? There are NO navigation buttons on this page to distract the prospect. In fact, there is only ONE action they can take - entering their contact information. Otherwise, they have to close the page completely... and if they do, THAT is when we can redirect them to the doctor's main website to see if there is something else that might grab their attention.

That informational offer provides them with proof that this doctor can actually get them the results they're looking for, and then within that information is an offer for

CHAPTER 4: MARKETING AND ADVERTISING

them to schedule a consultation with the doctor, which they are now more likely to do.

But consider these numbers for this doctor's <u>original</u> website. He could easily generate 300 or more leads per month using a pay-per-click campaign on Facebook. Those leads are then sent to his original website. He will then average around 10% of those leads. 30 prospects will see his offer for the free consultation and will call to <u>inquire</u> about it.

Notice I said INQUIRE about it, NOT request it. Out of that 10% who will call, only 10% of them will actually consent to the consultation, resulting in 3 prospects.

Fortunately, for most professionals like this doctor, they typically convert 100% of the prospects they get in front of, so those 3 prospects will more than likely become patients. Note that out of 300 leads, the doctor winds up with 3 new clients. That is the national average today – 1% of all leads generated will typically convert into a new client. That's pathetic!

But, now let's look at the doctor's new squeeze page. First of all, let's leave his number of leads at 300 per month. That squeeze page won't impact that number whatsoever. But let me ask you to think about this and give your open and honest opinion.

Do you think this new page will increase the number of prospects who will request this doctor's secrets to gaining and maintaining complete control of their child? The doctor was getting 10% with his old website. What percent do you think would request this new, more compelling offer?

Most responses I get average somewhere between 50% to 70%. Well, suppose we stay really conservative and say just 20% request the new offer.

That would mean 60 prospects would receive those secrets and actually see for themselves this doctor's methods really work.

And once they do, what percent of those do you think might request the consultation with the doctor? Remember, originally it was just 10%.

Again, most responses I get average between 50% to 70%. I would tend to agree with those numbers, but we know he originally converted 10%, so to be really conservative, let's just leave that conversion rate the same... 10%.

So, out of the 60 prospects requesting the doctor's secrets, 6 of them now request the consultation. And let's assume like we did originally the doctor converts all 6 of them into patients. That's an additional 3 patients per month, isn't it?

CHAPTER 4: MARKETING AND ADVERTISING

Now, let's say this doctor only charges $800 for his services, even though in reality it's typically 3 times that amount. $800 times 3 new patients is an additional $2,400 per month resulting in an annual increase of $28,800. That's obviously a dramatic increase in revenue considering we're being ridiculously conservative and all we did was make some slight changes to this doctor's website.

So, let me ask you this. Do you think we could get similar results for your business? How many leads have you generated in the last 12 months?

How many leads would you estimate you've generated this month? How many of those leads requested your offer? If we could create a similar process for your business and offer compelling information to your prospects just like we did for the child psychologist, do you think more prospects would respond? By what percent?

Could we <u>conservatively</u> agree a 10% opt-in rate is easily a no-brainer? Do you realize just one change alone would double your current sales revenue?

And that's assuming we don't increase your number of leads or your final conversion rate, which we will. If you said your last month's revenue was $25,000, then just this one change alone adds an additional $25,000 to your bottom line.

In a recent case study I conducted, I found $58,000 in additional annual revenue just using this one simple strategy.

But consider this!

That additional revenue is NOT just a one-time increase. That's revenue the business will generate year after year after year.

$58,000 in additional annual revenue increases the valuation of that business somewhere in the range of $150,000 - $200,000.

CHAPTER 5

Joint Ventures

Do you currently have any established joint venture partnerships?

JVs involve two or more businesses who decide to form a <u>partnership</u> to share markets or endorse a specific product or service to their customer base, usually under a revenue sharing arrangement. The key to creating successful joint ventures is to find partners who service the exact same type of clients who need or want what you sell.

Let me give you an example we're both familiar with - a florist. One of the most financially lucrative product lines for a florist is providing flowers for weddings. The average floral bill for a wedding often exceeds $3,000. But what we discovered about florists is they fall into what we refer to as an "event chain." An event chain simply refers to a series of businesses whose customers purchase in a specific sequence.

For example, a wedding will never take place until an engagement ring is purchased from a jeweler. So jewelers are at the forefront of every wedding chain. Once the young lady accepts the engagement ring, this event chain kicks into high gear. First, this young lady knows EXACTLY where she wants to get married, so number one on her agenda is to book the church, chapel, or synagogue where she wants the ceremony held.

Second on her list is to line up her wedding planner. Weddings today are a really big deal, and often women like to use the services of a professional wedding planner. Next up, she wants to secure the venue for her reception.

She knows most venues book out months in advance, so locking in that venue is high on her priority list. After that comes the wedding dress, so she begins the search for the perfect dress at an affordable price.

Next is our florist. The bride-to-be will want to begin selecting her floral arrangements for both the wedding and the reception. Then, after the florist comes the wedding cake, the printer for the invitations and thank you cards, and depending on the financial ability of the bride to be, she may also be interested in hiring a limo, a DJ for the reception, a travel planner for the honeymoon, the hotel, catering and so on.

This event chain is typical of this industry. And for the florist, it specifically identifies a multitude of potential and very lucrative JV partners. But here's why this becomes so important.

Every business ABOVE the florist has the potential to ENDORSE and SEND prospects to the florist. Unfortunately, the florist has NO control over that flow of prospects. Every business above the florist controls the JV relationship, so it's critical the florist create such a compelling offer and relationship with these businesses they feel <u>obligated</u> to send prospects their way.

But here's what's even better. The <u>florist</u> controls the prospect flow to ALL the businesses BELOW them in the chain, and by establishing specific processes and procedures to make sure their customers use those businesses, the florist can negotiate compelling offers with those business owners as well. So consider these numbers.

Let's say this florist cultivates a JV relationship with at least one of each business throughout this entire chain. Staying ultra-conservative with our estimates, would you agree this florist... since they have NO control over the flow of prospects from these businesses... is it likely they could obtain at least ONE referral each month from just <u>one</u> of the businesses above them?

OK, would you also agree conservatively since the <u>florist</u> controls the flow of prospects to the businesses BELOW them, they could easily send at least ONE referral to EACH one of them every month? Keep in mind these are VERY conservative estimates we're using here.

Since the average floral bill for a wedding is $3,000, ONE referral per month from the businesses ABOVE the florist increases their <u>annual</u> revenue by $36,000. Now let's consider the businesses BELOW the florist where the <u>florist</u> controls the referrals. Let's start with the wedding cake maker.

The average sales price for a wedding cake is also $3,000, and the florist could easily negotiate a 10% referral fee. So, just a <u>single</u> referral per month produces an additional annual increase of $3,600 for the florist.

Now consider the printer. The average sales price for printing is $1,000, and the florist again could receive a 10% referral fee, so that <u>single</u> referral per month produces an additional annual increase of $1,200.

If we stop there, this florist has just increased their annual revenue by more than $40,000, and that's using ridiculously conservative numbers. Imagine if you continued to add up the revenue produced by all the additional referral fees the florist would earn from all the other vendors in this chain.

This same process holds true for businesses that aren't in a chain. But just like the florist, they simply identify partners who service the exact same type of clients who need or want what they sell. Now I realize this looks easy, but it's not... and here's why.

You not only have to properly identify who would make an excellent joint venture partner for your business, but you also must determine the order to approach each one, how to approach them, and when to approach them. It's critical you do this properly or you wind up burning through all of your potential JV partners and come out with nothing in return.

Let me ask you a quick question. Just off the top of your head, how many potential JV partners would you estimate might be a fit for what you sell? Would you believe I could likely identify more than a dozen for your industry? So conservatively, how many referrals would you estimate might be possible if a dozen other businesses were compelled to refer their customers to you for additional purchases?

Conservatively, let's say you only get 3 referrals every month who buy from you. That's less than one per week. How much additional revenue would that add monthly? Now multiply that by 12 to see your annual revenue increase.

One more thing before we move on. Remember earlier we discussed the critical importance of creating a highly compelling informational offer promising so much value to prospects they would knock your door down to get it?

Suppose the florist offered this informational offer in their marketing, "5 Things Every Bride Should Know to Avoid Disaster on Their Wedding Day". This offer would place TONS of prospects into their drip campaign and result in a tremendous increase in sales. Those new sales can then be referred to their new JV partners and they collect multiple referral fees every month.

This would absolutely dwarf the revenue we just uncovered for the florist in this example. What I find really exciting about JVs is this is a strategy I help my clients implement immediately and it begins generating instant cash flow for them right out of the gate.

In a recent case study I conducted, I found $75,000 in additional annual revenue just using the JV strategy.

And again, that's revenue the business will generate year after year after year.

$75,000 in additional annual revenue increases the valuation of that business somewhere in the range of $225,000 - $300,000.

CHAPTER 6

Downselling

So far, we've only discussed 2 different lead generation strategies. Now let's discuss 2 lead-<u>conversion</u> strategies. We'll start with downselling. Do you currently use a downsell strategy?

Downselling is nothing more than offering a prospect an alternative product or service at a lower price when they decline your original offer. The goal is to turn the prospect into a client, so you not only realize some short-term financial benefit, but you gain the opportunity to do business with them again in the future.

For example, local health clubs always try to sell new members a full one-year membership. If that fails, they will try to downsell them by offering a 90-day "health makeover" membership. If that fails, they may go to a 30-day or possibly a one-week "trial" membership. They know if they can just get them to buy something the odds of them staying with them long term goes up exponentially.

Consider the florist. Most guys show up at a florist to buy roses for their better half. Valentine's Day, her birthday, their anniversary, Mother's Day and so on. But suppose a dozen roses cost $50 and the guy doesn't have that much money to spend. Since he has flowers on his mind, do you think he would consider an alternative that was just as romantic?

Do you realize if the alternative costs only $25, and the florist only used that downsell once each day, which is highly conservative, that would add almost $8,000 in annual revenue for them? And that's just one possible downsell opportunity. Suppose they had floral alternatives for weddings, lower priced options for funerals and so on.

What's your current price point for what you currently sell? Think you could come up with an alternative for half that price? How many of those would you conservatively estimate you could sell each week? Now multiply your reduced price times your number of weekly sales, then multiply that number times 52 weeks to reveal your annual increase.

And that's just one downsell. How many additional downsell opportunities would you conservatively estimate you could easily develop?

I recently found a business owner $65,000 in additional annual revenue through targeted downselling, and that additional revenue continues to grow year after year.

$65,000 in additional annual revenue increases the valuation of that business somewhere in the range of $200,000 - $230,000.

CHAPTER 7

Drip Campaigns

When a prospect doesn't buy what you sell, how many times do you follow up with them?

Small business owners focus primarily on generating leads. But remember that on average, less than 1% of prospects are NOW buyers. 99% are NOT ready to purchase that day, but many of them will buy sometime in the future, IF you continue to nurture them by staying in touch on an ongoing basis.

Unfortunately, the vast majority of small business owners rarely if ever follow up with their prospects after their initial contact with them. So why is that important? Listen to this VERY carefully! 80% + of ALL sales occur between the 5th and the 12th point of contact between the business and the prospect. 80%!!! Are you starting to see an opportunity here? This is where you need to implement a "drip campaign".

A drip campaign can add significant revenue to your business. It automatically delivers a form of communication to customers or prospects on a predetermined and scheduled basis. But here's the really cool part about this. Once you create your compelling offer, all you have to do is take specific segments from that offer and send it to your prospects on a consistent basis.

Let me show you an example of how this was done for a client who owned a sunroom company. When homeowners consider any type of remodeling project, whether it's their kitchen, an updated bathroom, or in this case installing a sunroom, wouldn't they love to get their hands on what you might call an "Idea Guide" featuring various models or state-of-the-art concepts?

Let me show you the Idea Guide developed for this sunroom company.

CHAPTER 7: DRIP CAMPAIGNS

Pretty impressive, wouldn't you agree? Well, would you like to hear the sad thing about this type of informational offer? Most prospects don't read it. They will request it with every intention of reading it, but only about 20% of them actually will. That's ok though, because it has already done its job, which was to compel the prospect to give us their contact information so we can begin our 5 to 12 touch points. And we simply use the information in the Idea Guide to do that quickly, efficiently, and inexpensively.

Here are a few examples for the sunroom company.

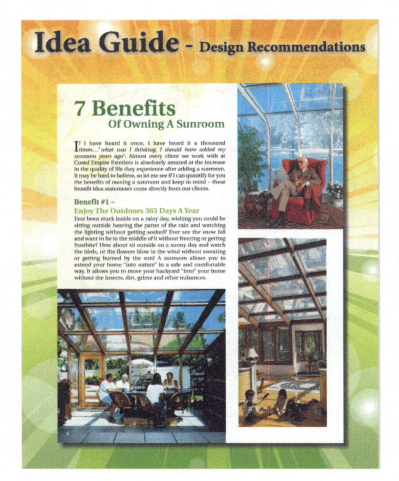

CHAPTER 7: DRIP CAMPAIGNS

Notice in the Idea Guide it starts out listing the 7 benefits of owning a sunroom. Benefit number one – enjoy the outdoors 365 days a year. Obviously, that's a HUGE reason someone would buy a sunroom, but unfortunately, 80% of prospects won't read that. So, let's reintroduce that benefit in our drip campaign and drive it home to the prospect. This sunroom company did that using a 6 X 11 oversized postcard, but they could have also done it through email.

Here's the postcard they sent out that emphasized this benefit.

CREATING A PROFIT SNOWBALL FOR YOUR BUSINESS

Notice benefit number 4 says owning a sunroom recharges your solar batteries.

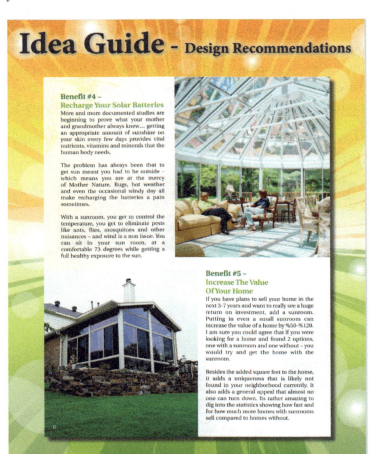

CHAPTER 7: DRIP CAMPAIGNS

Here's the postcard that emphasizes that benefit.

Benefit number 5 is major. It educates prospects on how a sunroom actually increases the value of their home. So, this postcard reinforces that fact.

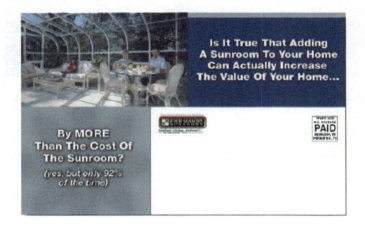

CHAPTER 7: DRIP CAMPAIGNS

But my point in showing you these is to emphasize that once you create your compelling informational offer, you pretty much have everything you need to implement your drip campaign. But look what begins to happen from the first day you start your drip campaign.

Let me go back to the child psychologist to show you the true impact of a drip campaign. If the child psychologist generated 300 leads per month, conservatively speaking we said he would average 60 prospects that would opt-in for his informational offer, and 6 of those 60 would become patients. So, that means 54 prospects did NOT buy his services.

Those are the prospects that now begin receiving the doctor's drip campaign. Out of those 54 prospects, an additional 2 of them will typically buy in the next 30 days. This is a pattern that continues month after month for as long as the doctor continues to stay in touch with these prospects and continues to offer them value. Every month 54 new prospects go into the top of the doctor's "funnel," and 2 additional sales per 54 prospects continues to be delivered from the bottom of the funnel.

Here's what the numbers look like over the first year.

54

54 + 52

54 + 52 + 50

54 + 52 + 50 + 48

54 + 52 + 50 + 48 + 46

54 + 52 + 50 + 48 + 46 + 44

54 + 52 + 50 + 48 + 46 + 44 + 42

54 + 52 + 50 + 48 + 46 + 44 + 42 + 40

54 + 52 + 50 + 48 + 46 + 44 + 42 + 40 + 38

54 + 52 + 50 + 48 + 46 + 44 + 42 + 40 + 38 + 36

54 + 52 + 50 + 48 + 46 + 44 + 42 + 40 + 38 + 36 + 34

54 + 52 + 50 + 48 + 46 + 44 + 42 + 40 + 38 + 36 + 34 + 32

At the end of year one, the doctor will have generated 3640 new prospects and 72 new clients through his squeeze page. But then the doctor produced a staggering 156 new clients through his drip campaign. And that's just year one!

This growth pattern continues year after year for as long as the doctor maintains this sales process. But here's the problem. By month 12 of year one, the doctor is generating 30

NEW patients every <u>month</u>. Is that a number this doctor can handle logistically? There's a limit on the number of patients this doctor can reasonably handle. When that number is reached, this doctor can literally STOP ALL lead generation efforts and let his drip campaign continue to produce additional patients far into the future.

Now let's calculate how this strategy will conservatively impact YOUR business. Remember, 80% of sales take place only AFTER 5 to 12 points of contact...and NONE of your competitors are doing anything like this whatsoever. Since you will be the only one in your market with this in place, you can logically expect to see a dramatic increase in both sales and conversions.

However, for the purpose of today's exercise, let's stay extremely conservative and calculate just a 10% conversion rate for your drip campaign. What were your total sales revenue last year? Whatever your number is, take 10% of that total. That's an <u>ultra</u>-<u>conservative</u> estimate of what a drip campaign can <u>easily</u> produce for your business over the next 12 months. That conservative amount can easily <u>double</u> each year, year after year, for as long as you keep your drip campaign in place. That's pretty exciting, isn't it?

During a recent business assessment, I found $120,000 in additional annual revenue by implementing a simple drip campaign... and that grows exponentially year after year.

$120,000 in additional annual revenue increases the valuation of that business somewhere in the range of $350,000 - $500,000.

CHAPTER 8

Upsell / Cross-sell

Let's move on to our third profit formula area. This involves increasing transactions with your prospects. In other words, getting them to buy from you more than they do now. There are 2 powerful revenue generating strategies that will work here.

Are you familiar with upselling and cross-selling? When you go to McDonald's and the kid behind the counter asks if you would like your meal "supersized," that's upselling. When that same kid then asks if you would like an apple pie to go with your supersized meal, that's cross-selling.

Upselling means offering a higher grade, quality, or size of the item the customer may be interested in at the point when the customer is ready to buy. Cross-selling means offering other products or services which <u>complement</u> the item the customer is interested in, at the point when the customer is ready to buy.

Now, here's what most business owners don't realize. 34% of prospects will buy additional products or services at the time of their original purchase IF they're asked to do so. Most businesses NEVER ask them, and they lose out on this lucrative opportunity to dramatically increase their revenue. Let me show you a brilliant example of this.

Up until about 3 years ago, most car owners on average paid around $29 to get their oil changed. Today, you can get your oil changed all day long for around $10. Take a look at this Groupon recently offered for 3 oil changes plus 3 additional services of your choice per visit.

CHAPTER 8: UPSELL / CROSS-SELL

The price for these today averages around $18. That's $6 per oil change, and then they add on an additional $4.50 for oil disposal, so the total for each oil change is less than $11. That's obviously a bargain. So why do they offer this when they used to get $29?

Simple... they finally realized the power of upselling and cross-selling, and they can't get the opportunity to upsell or cross-sell if they don't get themselves in <u>front</u> of their prospects. This Groupon is designed for <u>one</u> purpose only - to get them in front of as many prospects as possible - and the best way to do that is to give them what are basically free services.

But here's what most businesses don't understand about this strategy. This Econo Lube is breaking even by offering this Groupon. That $11 covers their material and labor costs. And those 8 free services you see listed along the bottom... you can select any 3 of them per visit... because Econo Lube is going to perform all of those services anyway. They know they make most of their profit through their higher-dollar service offerings, like batteries, brakes, transmission services, and repairs.

So, after the technician changes your oil, they're going to take all of your tires off so they can inspect your brakes... and cross-sell you a brake job. Since they have to remove all your tires to do that, why not offer you free tire rotation and a free brake inspection. Most of their patrons have no idea they're going to do this anyway, so they have this perception they're receiving all these services that they normally have to pay to have done... for free!

Notice Econo Lube offers to do a complete vehicle trip check where they do a complete inspection of your car before you take a long trip. A dealership would charge around $100 for that service, but Econo Lube includes 2 every 12 months. Well of course they want to do this. I guarantee you after checking over your entire vehicle, they WILL find SOMETHING wrong with your car. And since you're leaving on an extended trip, you will naturally want them to fix everything wrong. Are you starting to see the brilliance of this strategy?

So the key takeaway here for this strategy is to get yourself in front of your prospects as often as you can so you give yourself opportunities to sell them more. So let me show you how this exact same strategy will work for a dentist. Obviously, a dentist is about as far from an Econo Lube as you can get, but the principle is exactly the same... get in front of prospects and upsell / cross-sell them.

A dentist offers basic dental services like exams and teeth cleaning. That is NOT where they make their money. A

CHAPTER 8: UPSELL / CROSS-SELL

dentist generates the vast majority of their revenue from cosmetic services, root canals, crowns, fillings, and braces. So obviously the more patients they can get in front of, the more of these services they sell. The problem for dentists is that most people already have a dentist, and 90% of them will never change unless their dentist either retires or dies.

So what might convince someone to leave their current dentist? Consider these stats... 85% of the population have medical insurance, but only 50% have dental insurance. Among those without dental insurance, 44% said that was the main reason they didn't visit the dentist. See an opportunity here if you're a dentist?

What do you think might happen if a dentist specifically targeted families <u>without</u> dental insurance and offered them virtually the exact same services as those <u>with</u> dental insurance, but <u>without</u> paying the expensive monthly premiums? Here's a marketing campaign that was designed to do this for a dentist in Richardson, Texas.

CREATING A PROFIT SNOWBALL FOR YOUR BUSINESS

CHAPTER 8: UPSELL / CROSS-SELL

This obviously exploded this dentist's practice, but you might be thinking... how could he afford to offer this type of program? Same way the Econo Lube did!

The dentist basically offered patients routine services at his cost. That $25 covered the labor cost for the dental technician to take x-rays and clean the patient's teeth. But the dentist now had double the patients to upsell and cross-sell their more expensive and profitable services to. And of course, any business can always resort to the standard way to upsell and cross-sell customers - just make them more offers. A restaurant experiencing reduced revenue followed this advice.

They analyzed their profit margins on every one of their offerings, and determined their highest profit margin offerings were wine, appetizers, and desserts. They literally doubled their sales on all three of these by training the staff to offer them to every one of their patrons.

For example, they instructed their staff to bring an appetizer and wine cart to each table BEFORE the patrons ordered and offer free individual samples. Then, the staff repeated the same process at the end of each patron's meal by bringing the dessert cart around and giving a free sample of each dessert to everyone at the table as a way to entice patrons to order one of them. The taste and "reciprocity" instantly <u>doubled</u> their appetizer, wine, and dessert sales. But they didn't stop there.

CHAPTER 8: UPSELL / CROSS-SELL

The restaurant dramatically increased its <u>total</u> order revenue by implementing an <u>initial</u> order upsell strategy with the staff. They trained the servers to describe the more expensive entrées on the menu and give the patrons their personal recommendation. Most patrons have a tendency to go with the server's recommendations and this easily increased their total entree revenue by 15%.

So, let's assign a revenue figure for this strategy to your business. Remember, even a mediocre business can expect to see a 34% revenue increase by implementing this strategy. But since we want to be extremely conservative in our estimates, let's just factor in a 10% increase for your business. What's 10% of your annual revenue? That's what you could add to the bottom line of your business immediately using this strategy.

Just recently, I found $175,000 in additional annual revenue through a targeted upsell / cross-sell campaign.

$175,000 in additional annual revenue increases the valuation of that business somewhere in the range of $500,000 - $750,000.

CHAPTER 9

Expand Products or Service Offerings

Next, let's look at our second strategy for increasing transactions, and discuss how you could expand the number of products and services you offer. If you already provide a quality product or service, your current customers will be open to a variety of items you introduce, recommend, or endorse to them. Look, your current customers trust you, don't they? Then they will DEMAND additional products and services from you because they do trust you.

Unfortunately, most businesses don't have additional products or services to offer their client base, so you want to ask yourself, "what other products or services could my customers find valuable?" Once you make up a list of those offerings, go out and contact the providers of those offerings and set yourself up as an affiliate and negotiate a referral fee.

Consider a landscaper. As they make their clients' lawns and homes into a showcase, those homeowners may also need tree trimming, decking, fencing, stonework, a sprinkler system, outdoor lighting, a patio or outdoor kitchen installed, and perhaps a swimming pool.

The landscaper doesn't perform any of these services, but they are in a prime position to make professional recommendations, and most homeowners will go with those recommendations. The landscaper could easily negotiate anywhere from a 10% to 25% affiliate fee from each of these various service providers, and in the process, double their annual revenue.

I do this myself as a marketing strategist. My top tier clients receive a wide array of additional services I created for them. First, they get complete online access to all of my proprietary marketing and advertising, business growth training, strategies, tactics and resources 24/7/365 through an online E-Learning System I set up.

They receive weekly strategic marketing webinars where we teach them one specific strategy designed to immediately increase their revenue and profits. They gain access

CHAPTER 9: EXPAND PRODUCTS OR SERVICE OFFERINGS

to a weekly application workshop where I personally help them take the marketing strategy they just learned and show them how to implement it for their specific business. They also get a weekly Ask the Expert call with me where they can ask me ANY business related question they need answered, and then we meet once a month for an exclusive mastermind session where we find the group dramatic breakthroughs in both their sales and marketing efforts.

I also host for this group a monthly "lunch and learn". I created all of these additional services offerings myself, so these weren't something I had to go out and purchase. In fact, NONE of these services cost me a cent to develop or implement, but they are extremely attractive to a LOT of small business owners. They also do an excellent job of separating me from all of my competitors, because no one else I know offers anything even close to what I provide to my clients. My point being, we can do this for YOUR business as well.

How many additional offerings do you estimate you could be making right now? All you need to do is contact each service provider you identify and effectively negotiate a deal with them that's win-win. I would conservatively estimate this strategy will add an additional 10% of your current total revenue to your bottom line.

In a recent case study, I found $18,000 in additional annual revenue by simply offering additional products and services to their customer base.

$18,000 in additional annual revenue increases the valuation of that business somewhere in the range of $50,000 - $75,000.

CHAPTER 10

Bundling

Now let's check out a strategy for our fourth profit formula component - getting higher prices for what you sell. I like to use a "bundling" strategy here.

Bundling is simply the process of grouping together certain products to create packages which are then sold to clients. When you do this, you completely eliminate the biggest complaint small business owners have these days... competing on price.

Bundling removes price from the equation by creating an "apples to oranges" comparison. You have to remember customers today shop value - NOT PRICE! Unfortunately, small businesses are LOUSY at conveying their "value proposition", so therefore, price becomes the only value proposition left to consumers.

The real key to success in marketing is to offer more value than your competition. Prospects will pay twice the price if they believe they're receiving four times more value. Unfortunately, most businesses in a vain attempt to increase their value begin to offer discounts, and that often destroys their margins. Did you know if some businesses discount their price by a mere 10%, they now have to sell 50% more just to break even?

For example, if you sell a widget for $100, and you have a 30% profit margin, you make $30 for every widget you sell. That means your cost basis for that widget is $70. If you discount that widget 10% and sell it for $90 instead of $100, your cost basis is still $70. Now you're only making $20 in profit instead of $30.

For this business to make $1000 in profit selling their widgets at $100 each, they would need to sell 33.3 widgets ($30 X 33.3 widgets = $1000). But by discounting their price 10%, now they need to sell 50 widgets ($20 X 50 widgets = $1000). They now have to sell 50% more widgets just to get back to their original profit margin. (33.3 X 1.5 = 50).

But consider this... when was the last time you saw a business offer a measly 10% discount? Most of the time they offer 20% to 40% discounts and then scratch their heads wondering why they're going broke. And to add worse news on top of this already bleak scenario, did you know the latest research shows discounting doesn't actually impact a prospect's buying decision unless that discount is for 40% or more?

Want to know the closely guarded secret successful businesses DON'T want you to know?

STOP discounting!!! Instead, innovate your business so you offer more value than your competition... even if that means increasing your price. When you discount your price, you lose the full value of every dollar you discount. Bundling increases the perceived value, so prospects buy more.

Consider a home builder or remodeling contractor. They typically contract with certain suppliers who offer them huge volume discounts, especially for electronics. One builder agreed to buy multiple packages of a whole house entertainment system including a 50-inch television, a complete high-quality surround sound system, a complete home security system including surveillance cameras at all entry points to the home, and a complete fire protection and monitoring system.

The retail price for this package was $22,800 installed, but the builder acquired them in volume for around $6500 since installation would not be part of their costs. Since the builder already has the home stripped to the studs, installation can be handled during the actual project by their crew for pennies on the dollar. Now imagine this builder competing with other builders in a moderately priced neighborhood. All the builders offered homes in the $250,000 price range.

Our builder offered their home for $256,500 which included the additional $6500 out of pocket expense to the builder, and their home comes standard with a $22,800 home entertainment and full security system for FREE! Which builder would you buy from? In fact, what if this builder offered that new home for $260,000? Do you really believe that additional $3500 would prevent anyone from buying this home?

And does it still look like a MUCH better deal than the $250,000 home without the system? If the additional $3500 increase did make a difference due to loan qualification standards for certain prospects, the builder always has the option of reducing the price back to $256,500. They could even maintain their original price of $250,000 and lower their profit margin on each home sold.

This would allow them to possibly double their normal sales volume and practically double their overall profits every year. After all, they're still making around a 30% profit at $250,000. A home remodeler could use this same type of positioning for every remodeling job they bid on. Are you starting to see the potential here? Here's the marketing campaign developed for this builder.

CHAPTER 10: BUNDLING

But consider this fact. In the case of the builder, the home security and entertainment system weren't something they normally dealt with. It wasn't a product they typically carried.

They simply discovered this was something their prospects wanted to have included in the homes they were purchasing, so the builder went out and created an affiliate relationship with the home electronics provider and wound up doubling their sales and profits.

You just need to sit down and create a list of all the potential products and services you could bundle for YOUR business. This strategy can add substantial revenue for YOUR business. For the purposes of staying conservative in our estimates, let's do this. Bundling can easily increase any businesses revenue by 25% to 40%. Could we conservatively say you could easily expect to see a minor 10% revenue increase in your first year using this strategy? So, what does that translate to based on your current annual revenue?

In a recent case study, I found $26,000 in additional annual revenue through a coordinated bundling strategy.

$26,000 in additional annual revenue increases the valuation of that business somewhere in the range of $78,000 - $104,000.

CHAPTER 11

Increase Pricing

Now let's discuss our final profit formula component – more profit.

Obviously, there are 2 major ways to increase your overall profitability - increase revenue or decrease your cost of doing business. For now, let's discuss increasing your profitability. How about a really simple strategy – raise your prices. Most small businesses have NEVER raised their prices. That's because they don't know the facts when it comes to increasing their pricing. They're scared to death that ANY price increase, no matter how small, will lead to a mass exodus of all their customers. But is that really true?

Let's say you sell a widget for $100 and decide to increase that price 10% to $110. Will that small increase REALLY lead to a loss of customers? Honestly, I believe a few will leave, but they are most likely your biggest price shoppers that show NO loyalty or patronage to your business anyway. They will beat you down price-wise every chance they get, and the moment you begin to make a decent profit, they will leave you in a heartbeat for the next business willing to accept a financial beat down. But even though there will be some customer attrition, to what extent? Let's look at the numbers.

The business selling this widget is now making an additional $10; ALL of which is pure profit. Right there, that's a 33% profit increase. For this business to make $1000 in profit selling their widgets at $100 each, they would need to sell 33.3 widgets. But by increasing their price 10%, they only need to sell 25 widgets.

This means just to BREAK EVEN this business would have to LOSE 25% of its customers over a measly 10% price increase and that simply ISN'T going to happen! Of course, we need to perform a thorough price analysis on your business and determine the most lucrative price increase for you, but this is definitely a strategy I strongly recommend to all of my small business clients to help them increase revenue. There simply is no FASTER or EASIER way to generate additional revenue.

CHAPTER 11: INCREASE PRICING

Let me ask you a question. Do you think we might be able to increase your pricing by a meager 5% without running into any meaningful attrition? Let me put this into context for you.

Let's say you love to eat lunch at McDonald's, and your favorite meal is their Big Mac meal for $6.00. Today, you walk in at lunch to place that order, and the price has been increased to $6.25. Answer this honestly, would you even notice that price increase? And if you did notice, would it influence your decision to purchase that meal?

Of course not! That's less than a 5% increase – it's miniscule, and in most cases, it won't impact most businesses. You would have to be in an extremely price-sensitive market or industry for it to have any significant repercussions.

So, I strongly encourage you to 'test' a 5% price increase immediately. If it does have an impact, you can always revert back to your original price. Think about a business generating just $300,000 in revenue with a 40 gross profit margin.

A 5% price increase would generate an additional $15,000 in revenue and add $6,000 in gross profit. Total time invested – ZERO! Total effort required – ZERO! Risk factor for most businesses – NEGLIGIBLE!

Calculate what a 5% price increase would generate for your business and write it down. Whether your increase is 2%, 3% or 5%, the impact can be profound. But that's not even the best part...

CHAPTER 12

What the 1% Know

The best part is what the compounding impacts of the strategies in this book make collectively on your bottom line.

Consider all the revenue you've just identified throughout all of the strategies we have now covered. Keep in mind that number was decided on CONSERVATIVELY. And keep in mind this revenue ISN'T a one-time increase. This is revenue you will generate year after year after year as long as you diligently execute these strategies.

But here's the REALLY exciting news. Remember the snowball effect—the power of compounding impacts. Each strategy you add to your business builds and magnifies the impact of the other strategies, creating exponential growth! That means the true increase these strategies bring to your bottom line is not a question of addition but multiplication. To see what I'm talking about for your business, check out my online compounding impact calculator at: https://brauntrackbusinesstools.com/newprofit/

Make no mistake about it. Building the snowball effect in your business requires the right mindset. This requires perseverance and focus. Only the 1% of business owners who experience profitability breakthroughs are intentional about maintaining their mindset. The right mindset is established through 3 types of clarity: (1) values clarity; (2) goal clarity and (2) execution clarity.

Values Clarity: Being clear on your values is the foundation to why and how we do business. Personal values could range from things such as integrity, dependability, honesty to simplicity, courage or kindness. Having your values clarified is vital to giving you endurance to run the marathon of business through prosperous and difficult times. It also builds trust with your clients and customers.

Goals Clarity: Goals are powerful! They focus our attention, and energy on achieving desirable outcomes. Running a business is both time consuming and demanding. Therefore, the more defined your business goals are, the better chance you have of strategically investing your time on what really matters. Qualities of a powerful goal include it being specific, measurable, achievable and timely. Setting up the strategies in this book are great goals to have for your business to see its profitability increase exponentially.

Execution Clarity: Successful execution is the result of multiple decisions made daily which are determined by solid business information. To maintain the course toward exponential business growth, clarity tools are fundamental. Examples include establishing and following your own business scoreboard or working with a trusted business advisor who can help you stay on track. They will help you build strategic perspective, motivation, and accountability to keep you moving to seeing your business growth accelerate.

Working from crystal clarity is critical for you to realize exponential increases to your revenue. It's not complicated. However, when you execute each of these strategies, you've created a SYSTEM for your business that will generate a CONSISTENT, large number of leads, conversions and sales on an on-going basis. This systemization of your business creates a self-sustaining model that runs on its own WITHOUT you having to be there yourself. This is where you start to gain not only economic freedom but also freedom of time.

Consider this. If someone owns a website design company, every time they deliver a website to a client they have to go out and find a new client. It's never-ending for them. But when you execute these strategies, you will always have new orders in your pipeline thanks to compelling and powerful advertising coupled with your drip campaign. You will have JVs sending you revenue.

You will have upsells, downsells, and cross-sells taking place DAILY, along with selling additional affiliate products and services to your customers. You will implement higher pricing that your customers will WILLINGLY pay you thanks to the higher perceived value you've created. And you will have lower costs that will add significant revenue to your bottom line.

The only thing standing in your way now is getting all of this implemented in a timely and efficient manner. Please let me know if this is something you would like me to help you with.

Here's to your success!

Made in the USA
Monee, IL
28 March 2023